The ALASKAN PIPELINE

BY BENJAMIN LAZARUS

Scott Foresman
is an imprint of

Glenview, Illinois • Boston, Massachusetts • Chandler, Arizona
Upper Saddle River, New Jersey

Every effort has been made to secure permission and provide appropriate credit for photographic material. The publisher deeply regrets any omission and pledges to correct errors called to its attention in subsequent editions.

Unless otherwise acknowledged, all photographs are the property of Scott Foresman, a division of Pearson Education.

Photo locators denoted as follows: Top (T), Center (C), Bottom (B), Left (L), Right (R), Background (Bkgd)

Cover: ©Karen Kasmauski/Corbis; 1 ©Joel W. Rogers/Corbis; 3 ©Kimberly White/ Reuters/Corbis; 4 ©Bettmann/Corbis; 6–7 ©Staffan Widstrand/Corbis; 8 ©Bettmann/ Corbis; 9 ©Joel W. Rogers/Corbis; 10 ©Galen Rowell/Corbis; 11 ©Galen Rowell/Corbis; 12–13 ©Dan Guravich/Corbis; 14–15 ©Kennan Ward/Corbis; 16–17 ©Paul A. Souders/ Corbis; 18 ©Galen Rowell/Corbis; 19 ©Lloyd Cluff/Corbis; 20–21 ©Natalie Fobes/Corbis

ISBN 13: 978-0-328-51656-8
ISBN 10:   0-328-51656-2

OIL!

Without oil, we could not live as we do. Oil fuels most cars, trucks, buses, boats, trains, and planes. It fuels machines in factories. It heats homes, offices, and schools. Oil is used to make products such as ink, crayons, bubble gum, dishwashing liquids, ammonia, deodorant, eyeglasses,

phonograph records, and tires.

In 2003, the United States used 375.3 million gallons of oil a day for transportation and .468 million gallons of oil a day for other purposes. But the United States produces only 44% of the oil it uses. The rest is imported from other countries.

Importing oil from other countries is expensive. It's also risky. If there are problems in an oil-producing region, oil supplies can shrink and prices can climb. So American oil companies are always looking for ways to supply their own oil. They set up drilling sites all over the country to look for this valuable resource.

The pipeline promised to solve America's oil problem.

In 1968, oil companies discovered an enormous field of oil at Prudhoe Bay, on the northern coast of Alaska. Prudhoe Bay is above the Arctic Circle. It's far too remote for most forms of transportation. How would the oil companies get the oil to the rest of the United States?

THE PIPELINE

The answer was a pipeline. It would have to transport the oil 800 miles, to the port of Valdez. Valdez, though far south in the Gulf of Alaska, was the nearest ice-free port. There, oil could be loaded onto tankers and shipped to the rest of the United States.

Oil companies rushed to create a plan. They faced many challenges: They had to construct a pipe system to withstand the dramatic Alaskan climate, as well as Alaska's earthquakes. Oil would need to flow freely through the pipe. Since oil comes out of the ground hot, the heat generated in the pipe would need to be spread out. Heated pipes could harm the **permafrost**— a permanently frozen layer just below the surface of the ground. The oil companies were worried that if the permafrost melted, it could cause the pipe to sink and possibly break. The port of Valdez also had to be turned into a major shipping zone, capable of handling giant oil tankers.

ENVIRONMENTAL RISKS

But the idea of a pipeline crossing Alaska raised many questions. Some scientists and wildlife experts were concerned about the **environment**. They disagreed with the oil companies, believing that the impact of melted permafrost on a pipe was not the point. For them, the point was the danger of damaging the permafrost itself. Alaska's environment is fragile and interconnected. It sustains many forms of life. These, in turn, support and sustain each other. So harming one part of the environment could cause major damage to other parts.

Some environmental experts asked what would happen to this special world if there were an accident. What damage would an oil spill do? What about the effects of roads and trucks? Some people believed the enormous construction project was simply too much for the Alaskan environment.

Others, however, believed the pipeline was a terrific idea with little risk. They argued that the pipe would be well constructed and the chance of accidents would be extremely low. They believed that the effects of roads and trucks on the land would be minor. Finally, they argued that the tremendous benefits to the entire country greatly outweighed any possible risks.

In 1970, people fought to halt the project with a series of lawsuits. They argued that the pipeline would have lasting effects on Alaska's environment. They requested that the oil companies find less destructive ways to transport the oil.

But the oil companies insisted that they could make sure the pipeline was harmless. They argued that every day spent trying to halt the pipeline was costing the United States millions in foreign oil payments.

The environmentalists lost. In 1973, President Richard M. Nixon signed the Trans-Alaska Pipeline Authorization Act. By 1974, construction was underway.

CONSTRUCTION

When it was built, the pipeline was the most expensive, privately funded project of its kind. It cost 8 billion dollars. Creating a marine terminal at the port of Valdez cost $1.4 billion. Creating the pipeline required five separate contracting companies and a crew of 21,000

people. Twenty-nine temporary camps were built. Three million tons of material were shipped to the construction sites. Fourteen airfields were built to transport crew and materials.

The pipe itself is steel and measures 48 inches in diameter. It is built in six separate sections that, when connected, run 799 miles from northern to southern Alaska. It crosses three mountain ranges and more than 800 rivers and streams. Some parts are buried underground.

Engineers worked to find solutions to the challenges of placing the pipeline in the Alaskan climate. The pipeline is built in a zig-zag so it can naturally expand and contract, depending on outside temperatures. To keep oil moving, 12 pumping stations were built along the pipeline. To help prevent the oil's heat from melting the permafrost, radiators to spread the heat out were installed.

The pipeline was finally completed in June 1977. That August, oil began to flow. The first tanker to ship pipeline oil from the port of Valdez was the *ARCO Juneau*. Since then, some 16,000 tankers have been filled at Valdez, and more than 13 billion barrels of oil have traveled through the pipeline. Daily, the pipeline can transport up to 2.1 million barrels. That's a lot of oil.

But were the oil companies right? Has the pipeline been a success with minimal damage to the environment? Or were the environmentalists right? Were Alaska's landscape and wildlife harmed? Was the Alaskan environment changed forever?

What would the pipeline do to the untouched beauty of the Alaskan

Winters on the Alaskan tundra are long, and summers are short. But animals that live there have adapted to its environment. In fact, it would be harder for them if conditions change.

ALASKA'S ENVIRONMENT

To understand the relationship between the pipeline and the Alaskan environment, it's important to understand what makes Alaska so unique.

Alaska is an enormous state. At its widest points, it measures 1,400 miles from north to south and 2,700 miles from east to west. Its landscape includes mountain ranges, glaciers, fjords, bays, streams and rivers, island chains, and vast stretches of land. It has many different regions and climates. Some regions are covered with snow and ice most of the time. Other regions are heavily forested, with a dense **canopy** high over the forest floor. Still others are a combination of mountains, sloping fields, and flat lands.

Top layer of soil, permafrost

Dangerous gases are frozen.

If the permafrost is disturbed, the dangerous gases frozen beneath the surface can be released into the environment.

Much of northern Alaska is known as the tundra. The **tundra** may look like a frozen wasteland, but it's not. It's a **wondrous** system of seasonal freezing and thawing that supports hundreds of different species of wildlife and plants. The tundra includes a surface layer of soil that can be as deep as six inches. Below that is the permafrost layer.

The permafrost is an extremely important part of the tundra for many reasons. It keeps the ground in place and makes it stable. It keeps dangerous gases frozen beneath the surface so that they are not released into the air, water, or soil. These gases include carbon dioxide and methane. The permafrost also helps rain drain into rivers and streams, keeping waterways full of fresh water.

A Living Paradise

The animals living on the tundra include foxes, caribou, grizzly and polar bears, ducks, and snowy owls. They are able to survive the region's long winters and short, cool summers. When temperatures rise in the summer, the layer of soil on the surface of the tundra bursts into life. **Lichens** dapple once-bare rocks. Valleys fill with flowering plants, mosses, and shrubs. Those plants depend on seasonal freezes in order to come back to life every spring. Then the air is **fragrant** with wildflowers. Fields of wildflowers are buzzing with bees, which **pollinate** flowers as they collect their **pollen**.

Alaskan wildlife includes salmon, moose, black-tailed deer, caribou, mountain goats, wild sheep, bears, wolves, harbor seals, porpoises, dolphins, humpback and minke whales, sea lions, sea otters, and walruses. Alaska is also home to more than 400 species of birds, from the tiny sparrow to the great bald eagle. In addition, thousands of migratory birds come to Alaska each spring.

Alaska's plant life changes, depending on the region. Alaska is home to 33 native tree species, including the Sitka spruce, western hemlock, alder, white spruce, cottonwood, and paper birch. The mosses, wildflowers, and other plants (some underwater) that grow in various regions provide vital food for fish, birds, and animals.

A polar bear crosses the ice.

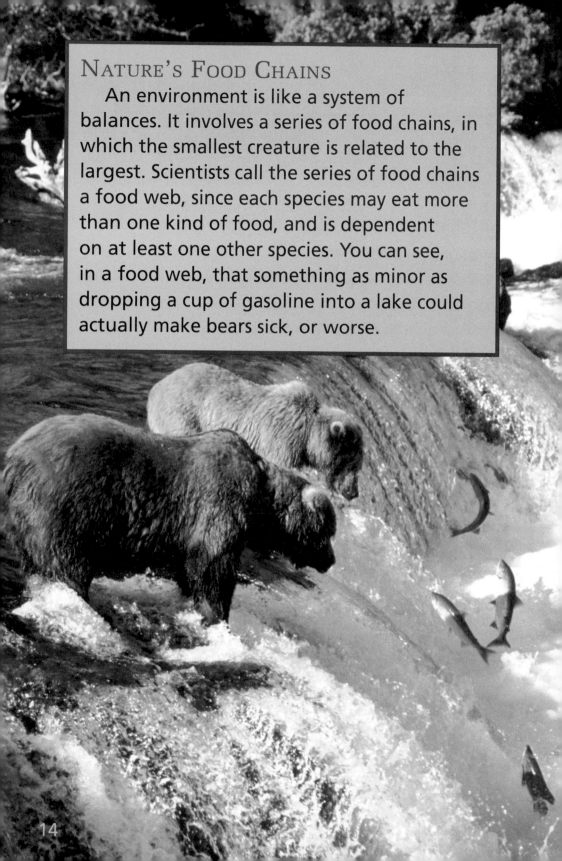

Nature's Food Chains

An environment is like a system of balances. It involves a series of food chains, in which the smallest creature is related to the largest. Scientists call the series of food chains a food web, since each species may eat more than one kind of food, and is dependent on at least one other species. You can see, in a food web, that something as minor as dropping a cup of gasoline into a lake could actually make bears sick, or worse.

An Underwater Food Chain

Imagine one aspect of the food web in the water along the Alaskan coast:

1. The cold, unpolluted arctic waters provide an ideal home for healthy marine organisms, such as plankton and algae.
2. Tiny fish feed on the organisms.
3. Larger fish feed on the smaller fish.
4. Seals feed on the larger fish.
5. Whales and polar bears feed on the seals.

A Food Chain on Land

Now let's take a close look at life on the tundra of northern Alaska. Here's how one link of the food chain affects another:

1. Summer's warming temperatures create vast fields of wildflowers, grasses, and shrubs across the tundra.
2. The plant life provides homes and food for insects, such as flies and bees.
3. Nesting and breeding birds feed on the plentiful supply of insects.
4. The birds, with enough food to thrive, reproduce and lay their eggs.
5. Some of the eggs provide food for predators, such as foxes and bears.
6. The predators, with enough food to thrive, reproduce and give birth to the next generation.

THE PIPELINE'S IMPACT

Has any aspect of the Trans-Alaska Pipeline damaged Alaska's environment? Have there been any accidents? Has the pipeline been running normally? Let's take a closer look at one important part of the working pipeline system: roads.

THE IMPACT OF ROADS

Hundreds of miles of roads had to be built in Alaska to transport crews and materials to the pipeline project. To create the roads, parts of the landscape had to be plowed and graded.

Part of this landscape includes miles and miles of Alaskan tundra. When thawed, this tundra works like a giant system of tiny water channels. Water flows freely through these channels. It fills watering holes for animals, and provides plants with vital nutrients. Additionally, the plants provide food for some of these animals. These grazing animals provide food for other animals.

But the pipeline roads have, in fact, damaged the water system on the tundra. In some places, creating a road has cut off the flow of water. In other places, creating a road caused too much water to flow in that area, which resulted in flooding. You can continue the cause-and-effect: Flooding kills the plant supply. Fewer plants means less food for animals, resulting in a decrease in the animal population.

A second effect of roads is damage to the thin layer of soil over the permafrost. This soil is home to countless species of plants in the spring and summer. It also provides shelter to many animal species. If soil is damaged, the plants can't grow. Again, if plants can't grow, animals can't eat. That's a simplification of a complicated process, but it shows that the roads do have an impact on the wildlife.

The oil companies that built the pipeline had to build an entire network of roads to supply and maintain it.

Roads were constructed across the fields where herds of caribou had fed for generations. The roads reduced the food supply by damaging the soil. As a result, the caribou herds could not get enough to eat.

A third effect involves the chemicals used to build the roads. During the rainy season, those chemicals were washed from the roadbed into the soil. Once in the soil, they spread out. Plants were killed when they came into contact with these chemicals. Minerals the plants use for nutrition were damaged by the chemicals, which also harmed the plants. As groundwater flowed into streams, the chemicals in the ground flowed into those streams as well. Fish were affected. Animals that ate the fish were also affected.

Landslides in Alaska happen when the solid layer of ice on the ground melts. The condition is called thermokarst.

THERMOKARST

The roads have had another effect across much of the entire surface of Alaska. They have created a condition called **thermokarst**.

Thermokarst means that the solid layer of ice on the ground has melted. This can happen because of melting snow on the pipeline roads. When the snow melts on the roads, it leaks into the ground and melts the ice beneath the surface. When this ice melts, the ground caves in. Ruts, tunnels, mounds, and valleys form.

Under the wheels of tractors and construction vehicles, thermokarst gets worse. When the roads were built or repaired, heavy-tired vehicles created deeper holes and valleys in the fragile ground. Along the coast, thermokarst eroded the shoreline, causing the sea level to rise. That has damaged nesting and breeding sites of some migratory birds.

Thermokarst has a clear cost to humans as well. As the land becomes more unstable, landslides result. In one case, a landslide destroyed an entire Native American village. In another, it swallowed up runways at the airport in the city of Fairbanks.

ACCIDENTS

The environmental damage caused by thermokarst can be repaired. But experts say it will take at least a billion dollars. Billions of dollars have also been spent dealing with another effect of the pipeline, accidents.

Accidents in the pipeline cause oil to spill into the environment. Oil, a harsh pollutant, harms living things all the way up the food chain. If ingested, oil is poisonous. But even contact with it can kill an organism. Oil in the water can suffocate fish by clogging their gills. It coats whales' and porpoises' blowholes, making it impossible for them to breathe. On land, it can coat birds, mammals, and their food and homes.

No one could promise that there would be no accidents on the pipeline. In fact, there were many. But some accidents made front-page news. In February 1979, an explosion in a pipe caused a spill of over 16,000 barrels of oil. In 2001, a hunter shot a bullet into a pipe's connecting weld, causing another leak. But back in 1989, an accident took place that turned into a major environmental tragedy.

The *Exxon Valdez* oil spill took place in 1989.

The *Exxon Valdez* Disaster

On March 24, an oil tanker called the *Exxon Valdez* began its journey out of port. The new ship was 987 feet long, with 11 cargo tanks and a crew of 19. It was carrying a full load of oil. A little after midnight, it ran into an underwater reef. The impact ripped into the hull. Eight cargo tanks were torn open. Within hours, 11 million gallons of oil spilled into Prince William Sound. Within two months, 500 miles of Alaskan coastline was covered in oil.

Immediately, many thousands of fish, sea birds, and sea mammals began to die. In the weeks and months to come, deaths increased. Emergency crews from around the world raced to save the oil-coated wildlife. Hospitals were set up to clean creatures as big as whales and as small as sparrows.

The accident showed how unprepared the tanker's owners were for such a major spill. It took three years before intensive clean-up began. In 1994, a jury ordered the owners to pay $5 billion in fines. The tragedy proved that the pipeline project was indeed full of risk.

Prince William Sound may never fully recover. Of the dozens of species of wildlife that suffered damage, some are still weakened. Populations have shrunk. In some species, the young have crippling birth defects. But other species are recovering.

Now Try This

Go to the library or use the Internet to learn more about Alaska. You may want to have a parent or teacher help you find the best Web sites or materials. Then, pick a topic related to Alaska and the pipeline. It can be

- Native American tribes in Alaska
- Wildlife conservation in Alaska
- Climate change in Alaska
- Finding new sources of energy besides oil

1. Research your topic to get another part of the pipeline story. Write down 10 key points on the information you found. Then consider this: How has the presence of the pipeline affected what you researched? For instance, did it cause an improvement? Did it cause a harmful change? Did it inspire more work done in the field?

2. Take your findings and your research and consider what you learned in this book. Now it's time to make a general decision and then write.

3. Write two paragraphs:
   In the first paragraph, write your decision: What do you think about the pipeline? Did you decide it was a good idea? a bad idea? a mixed idea?
   In the second paragraph, write about how your research helped you come to your decision. Did your research support your first impression? Or did it change your mind?

Glossary

canopy *n.* a cover formed by the leafy upper branches of trees in a forest.

fragrant *adj.* having a pleasant scent.

environment *n.* the area in which something exists or lives.

lichens *n.* a plant that is a combination of algae and fungus, usually found in crusty patches on rocks or ground.

permafrost *n.* a permanently frozen layer of soil.

pollen *n.* the fertilizing element of flowering plants.

pollinate *v.* to convey pollen from flower to flower.

thermokarst *n.* a landscape where many small pits are formed by the melting of ground ice, or permafrost.

tundra *n.* a treeless plain typical of the arctic and subarctic regions.

wondrous *adj.* wonderful; remarkable.